NOAH and GOD'S PROMISES

Genesis 6—8
for Children

W9-BAB-176

Written by Gloria A. Truitt
Illustrated by Jules Edler

Publishing House
St. Louis

ARCH® Books
Copyright © 1985 CONCORDIA PUBLISHING HOUSE
3558 S. Jefferson Avenue, St. Louis, MO 63118-3968
Manufactured in the United States of America

Noah was a godly man
  Who lived quite long ago;
And you can read about his life
  In Genesis, you know.

Now, Noah's family never strayed
  From God as others had;
Although God loved this family,
  The others made Him sad.

Except for Noah's family,
All people loved their sin;

Though once their hearts were filled with love,
  Now evil ruled within.

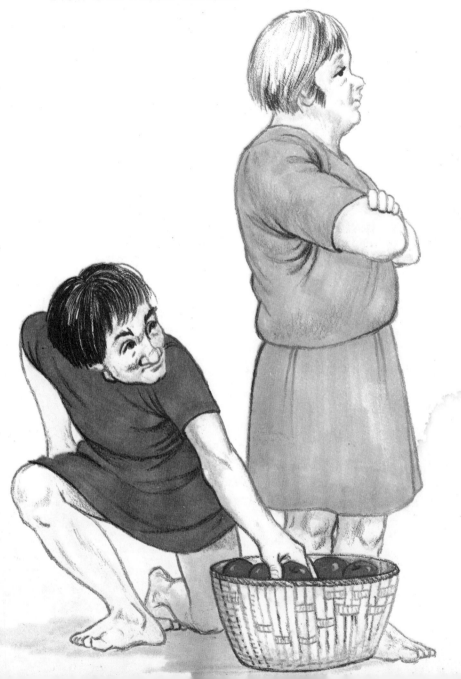

So God decided what to do;
    He came up with a plan:
With water He'd destroy all flesh—
    All beasts, all birds, and man.

But Noah, in his faith-filled life,
    Was favored in God's eyes,
So God said, "Noah, I'll save *you*,
    Your *sons* and *all your wives*."

God said to Noah, "Build an ark,"
Then told him how to do it.
The Lord's instructions were exact,
Right down to the last cubit.

And then the Lord said, "When it's done,
 Please follow My design:
Bring in each animal and bird,
 A pair of every kind."

Upon the day the ark was done
The families went inside;
Then came the animals and birds
As God had specified.

Two by two they filed aboard
Before the flooding rain
Would cover every living thing
From mountaintop to plain.

The thunder boomed, the lightning streaked
Through storm clouds thick and dark,
But Noah's family, beasts, and birds
Were snug inside the ark.

The waters filled the valleys deep
And climbed the mountain heights
While Noah's family waited out
Those forty days and nights.

Old Noah was a faithful man.
  He knew that by-and-by
The rains would stop and all the land
  Would once again be dry.

So when the rains had ended, and
The sun began to shine,
He sent a dove to search the earth
And carry back a sign.

An olive branch proclaimed dry land,
    So Noah's family knew
That they could leave the ark quite soon—
    And all the creatures, too.

Old Noah waited patiently
　　Until God spoke the word:
"Go out and take along with you
　　Each animal and bird."

Upon a mount called Ararat
    They offered thanks in prayer
To God who saved them from the flood
    With His great loving care.

Now, God was pleased to see the praise
    Of Noah and his crew,
So God announced upon that day
    His promise ever true:

"I'll never bring a flood again
    To cause all flesh to die;
The symbol of My vow will be
    A rainbow in the sky."

Now when the storm clouds gather, and
Big raindrops start to fall,
We do not have to be afraid . . .
God's promise we'll recall.

The sun will shine! God told us so!
   And through those shining rays
We'll see His sign, the rainbow, and
   To God we'll offer praise.

DEAR PARENTS:

The rainbow is a visible reminder of God's promise never again to destroy the world with a flood. "As long as the earth endures," God said to Noah, "seedtime and harvest, cold and heat, summer and winter, day and night will never cease. . . . Whenever the rainbow appears in the clouds, I will see it and remember the everlasting covenant between God and all living creatures of every kind on the earth" (Gen. 8:22; 9:16 NIV).

God has "remembered" another of His promises, too. It is a promise He first made to Adam and Eve in the Garden (Gen. 3:15) and one He later renewed with Abraham, Isaac, and the family of Israel: "I will bless you; . . . and all peoples on earth will be blessed through you" (Gen 12:2-3 NIV).

The fulfillment of that promise is Jesus Christ, God's Son. Through Noah, God saved the earth from complete desolation; through the death of His own Son, God provided a way of salvation for all from a kind of desolation far worse than any a flood can bring—eternal death and separation from Himself.

Whenever you see a rainbow, remind your child of God's great love for everyone. He loves us so much that He sacrificed His own Son so that we might share eternal life with Him.

THE EDITOR